*Wanderlust Bucketlist Series*

# Discover Arizona

## Travel Guide, Adventure Game Plan, and Wish List

John Christopher Lee

www.pemaquidbooks.com

graphics by BirDIYdesign

(subject to an unlimited commercial license)

# Table of Contents

# INTRODUCTION

**Have you ever stood on the edge of a canyon so vast it seems to stretch into eternity, with colors so vivid they appear to be painted by the hand of an artist? Or wandered through a desert that comes alive with blooming wildflowers after a rare rain? If you haven't, let me tell you—Arizona is unlike anywhere else.**

Arizona is a land of contrasts. From snow-capped peaks to sun-scorched deserts, ancient cultures coexist with vibrant modern cities. This isn't just a state; it's a journey through time, nature, and human ingenuity. There's magic here—something about how the sunsets paint the sky in fiery oranges and purples, how the saguaro cacti stand tall like silent sentinels, and how the air smells fresh and wild. Arizona doesn't just offer adventures; it provides transformation.

## The Allure of Arizona

Arizona is a state that defies expectations. Take the Grand Canyon, for example. Standing on its rim is a humbling experience, a reminder of how small we are in the face of nature's grandeur.

But Arizona isn't just about its famous spots. There are countless hidden gems for every well-known destination—places you can only find by veering off the beaten path, conversing with a friendly local, or taking a chance on a dirt road.

Arizona's history is as rich as its landscapes. From the ancient cliff dwellings of the Ancestral Puebloans to the vibrant art scene in Sedona, there's a story behind every corner. Native American heritage is woven deeply into the fabric of the state, and you'll find opportunities to learn about it everywhere—from museums and guided tours to festivals and traditional ceremonies.

## Best Times to Visit and Seasonal Highlights

Arizona is a year-round destination, but knowing when to visit can make all the difference. In the spring, the desert blooms come alive with color, and the weather is perfect for hiking. Fall brings cooler temperatures and a golden glow to the aspens in Northern Arizona.

Summer, while hot, isn't off-limits—it's the perfect time to explore higher elevations or cool off at one of the state's many lakes. In winter, you can ski in Flagstaff in the morning and enjoy a sunny hike in the desert in the afternoon.

## Journey Awaits

As you embark on your Arizona adventure, know you're stepping into a world of endless possibilities. This isn't just a trip; it's an invitation to connect with nature, history, and yourself in ways you never imagined. Whether you're marveling at the majesty of the Grand Canyon, exploring a ghost town, or simply watching the stars in one of the state's many dark-sky parks, Arizona has a way of staying with you long after you've left.

# CHAPTER 1

## Northern Arizona Wonders

---

*"In every walk with nature, one receives far more than he seeks." – John Muir*

---

**Northern Arizona is a land of breathtaking contrasts and absolute beauty. It is where ancient history meets adventure, where the earth reveals its secrets through majestic canyons, windswept mesas, and towering peaks.**

Whether you're seeking awe-inspiring landscapes, cultural experiences, or the kind of adventures that make your heart race, this region offers it all in abundance. Let's start our journey in one of the most iconic destinations in the world—the Grand Canyon National Park.

## Exploring the Grand Canyon National Park

If there's one place that truly defines the essence of Northern Arizona, it's the Grand Canyon. No matter how many photos you've seen or stories you've heard, nothing can prepare you for the moment you stand on the edge of the South Rim and take in the vastness of this natural wonder.

The Grand Canyon is not just a place you visit; it's a place you experience. The South Rim is a perfect starting point with its sweeping views and well-maintained trails. Begin your journey at the Grand Canyon Visitor Center, where you'll find maps, exhibits, and knowledgeable staff ready to help you plan your day.

If you're up for a stroll, the Rim Trail offers spectacular views without requiring strenuous effort. For a deeper dive, the Bright Angel Trail provides an unforgettable trek into the canyon's depths.

The Grand Canyon is a haven for adventure seekers. Guided rafting trips range from half-day excursions to multi-day adventures that immerse you in the canyon's wild beauty.

For a more serene experience, consider a mule ride along the canyon trails. These gentle giants have safely transported visitors through the Grand Canyon for over a century. Riding a mule down the narrow, winding paths is exhilarating and offers a unique perspective on the canyon's immense scale.

The Grand Canyon is a treasure trove of history. The Desert View Watchtower, designed by architect Mary Colter in 1932, is a tribute to Native American artistry. You'll find murals that tell the story of the region's indigenous peoples.

You should consider a guided tour of the Grand Canyon. Whether it's a ranger-led hike, airplane-guided adventure, or a helicopter ride over the canyon, having an expert by your side can add context to your experience.

The Grand Canyon is a place to be savored. Sit on the rim with a journal, take in the view, and let the grandeur of this natural wonder seep into your soul.

## Antelope Canyon and Horseshoe Bend Adventures

There's magic in the way light dances. You'll find this magic in Antelope Canyon, where the sun's rays transform narrow sandstone walls into glowing, dreamlike passages. Located just outside Page, Arizona, this slot canyon is one of the most photographed places in the world—and for good reason.

Your adventure begins with a guided tour, the only way to access the Upper and Lower sections of Antelope Canyon. In the Upper Canyon, shafts of sunlight stream down from above, creating surreal patterns and illuminating the rock's reds and oranges. The Lower Canyon, narrower and more challenging to navigate, offers equally stunning views with a slightly more adventurous twist.

A short drive away is Horseshoe Bend, a breathtaking overlook of the Colorado River as it makes a dramatic 270-degree curve. This iconic site, often called the "East Rim of the Grand Canyon," is easily accessible via a short hike from the parking area.

Antelope Canyon and Horseshoe Bend are connected to the Navajo Nation, and visiting these sites offers an opportunity to learn about the region's rich cultural heritage. Many guides who lead tours through Antelope Canyon are members of the Navajo community.

## Monument Valley and Navajo Tribal Park Insights

Nestled within the Navajo Nation, Monument Valley is a stunning natural wonder and a place steeped in history and culture. As you approach the valley, the towering red rock formations seem to rise out of the earth, their stark beauty contrasting with the desert sky.

Your first stop should be the Monument Valley Navajo Tribal Park Visitor Center. From here, you'll get your initial glimpse of some of the valley's most famous formations, including the Mittens and Merrick Butte.

The best way to truly immerse yourself in the valley is by taking a guided tour led by a Navajo guide. These tours offer access to areas off-limits to the general public, including ancient ruins, petroglyphs, and sacred sites. The guides share stories and legends passed down through generations, giving you a deeper understanding of the land and its significance to the Navajo people.

For a more adventurous experience, consider hiking or horseback riding in the valley. The Wildcat Trail is the only self-guided hiking trail in the park, offering a closer look at the Mittens. On the other hand, horseback riding allows you to channel your inner cowboy or cowgirl as you explore the desert landscape.

Monument Valley is also rich in cultural experiences. If you have the chance, attend a Navajo cultural event or demonstration. From traditional hoop dancing to rug weaving, these events provide a glimpse into the vibrant heritage of the Navajo people. And don't leave without trying fry bread—a delicious staple of Navajo cuisine.

## Flagstaff and the Scenic San Francisco Peaks

Flagstaff is the kind of place where the Old West meets modern adventure. Nestled at the San Francisco Peak bases, this charming mountain town is a gateway to Northern Arizona's most breathtaking natural wonders.

Driving into Flagstaff, you'll notice the towering peaks dominating the skyline. These are the San Francisco Peaks, sacred to many Native American tribes, including the Hopi, Navajo, and Zuni. Humphreys Peak is 12,633 feet, the tallest point in Arizona. If you're up for a challenge, hiking to the summit offers incredible views.

The Arizona Snowbowl is a fantastic destination. It transforms into a snowy playground for skiing and snowboarding in the winter. But even in the warmer months, the Snowbowl offers scenic chairlift rides that provide panoramic views of the surrounding forests and valleys.

Downtown Flagstaff is a delightful mix of old and new. Historic Route 66 runs right through the heart of town, and you can't miss the vintage signs and classic diners that harken back to a bygone era. A favorite spot is the Weatherford Hotel, a historic landmark with a cozy bar and a rooftop patio perfect for soaking in the mountain air.

Flagstaff is also an outdoor enthusiast's paradise. The nearby Coconino National Forest boasts diverse landscapes, from ponderosa pine forests to red rock canyons. The Lava River Cave, a unique underground tube formed by ancient volcanic activity, is a must-visit for anyone with a sense of adventure.

The Lowell Observatory is a hit for all ages. Known as the place where Pluto was discovered, this observatory offers exhibits and nightly stargazing programs. On a clear night, the telescopes give you an up-close view of planets, star clusters, and galaxies.

## Northern Arizona Bucketlist

### 1. Coal Mine Canyon

Tucked between Tuba City and Cameron, Coal Mine Canyon is a stunning kaleidoscope of layered colors. Visit during sunrise or sunset for an almost otherworldly glow and bring a sense of wonder—you won't find crowds here.

**2. Blue Canyon on Hopi Land**

Blue Canyon is sacred, quiet, and ethereal, accessible only with a guide or permit from the Hopi Nation.

**3. Horseshoe Bend Overlook (Secret Spot)**

This is the less trafficked overlook about 2 miles away. While the leading site teems with visitors, this secret spot lets you experience the grandeur of the Colorado River without the crowds.

**4. Grand Falls (aka Chocolate Falls)**

Known as the "Niagara Falls of the Southwest," Grand Falls is a seasonal wonder that comes alive in spring when rain and snowmelt feed the Little Colorado River. Its muddy waters cascade 185 feet—higher than Niagara itself.

**5. Jerome Ghost Town**

Perched high atop Cleopatra Hill, Jerome is an old mining town turned ghostly retreat and boasts hidden alleys, abandoned buildings, and the nearby Gold King Mine Museum.

**6. Sycamore Canyon Wilderness**

The lesser-known sibling of Oak Creek Canyon, Sycamore Canyon, is rich in wildlife, ancient cliff dwellings, and secluded trails.

### 7. Little Painted Desert County Park

If you're mesmerized by the Painted Desert but dislike crowded observation points, drive to this lesser-visited park near Winslow, Arizona.

### 8. The Wave's Neighboring Wonders

The surrounding Vermilion Cliffs offer otherworldly rock formations just as magical and far less crowded. White Pocket, for example, boasts swirling sandstone formations that look like petrified waves frozen in time.

### 9. Antelope Canyon's Fjords (Canyon X)

Skip the overcrowded Upper and Lower Antelope Canyons and visit Canyon X instead. This quieter section offers identical dramatic light beams and narrow, sculpted walls but with fewer tourists vying for the perfect Instagram moment.

### 10. Walnut Canyon Cliff Dwellings

While Sedona captures much of the region's spiritual attention, the ancient cliff dwellings of Walnut Canyon near Flagstaff tell a story of resilience and adaptability.

### 11. Devil's Bridge at Sunrise (Without the Crowds)

While Devil's Bridge has grown in popularity, catching the sunrise here offers an entirely different experience. Arrive before the crowds, and you'll have the iconic rock arch.

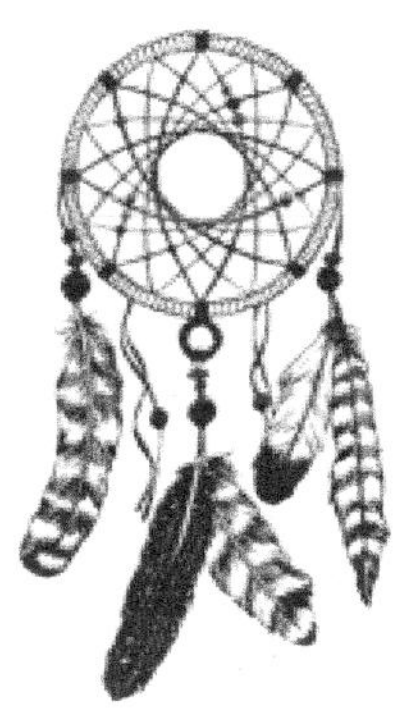

# CHAPTER 2

# Sedona's Spiritual Vibes and Red Rock Wonders

---

*"Sedona is a cathedral without walls. It is a place where the earth speaks to you, and the sky listens." – Unknown*

---

**Sedona isn't just a destination; it's a feeling, an experience, a place that captures your soul and invites you to explore its stunning landscapes and yourself. Nestled in the heart of Arizona, Sedona is renowned for its red rock formations, vibrant art scene, and legendary energy vortexes.**

Sedona offers the answer if you've ever wondered what it's like to stand at the intersection of natural beauty and spiritual wonder. Locals and visitors speak of a unique energy that pulses through the region, a magnetic pull that draws people in and changes them.

## Sedona's Energy Vortexes

When people think of Sedona, the term "energy vortex" often comes to mind. The concept of energy vortexes stems from the belief that certain areas on Earth are natural power centers where energy is either entering or leaving the ground. In Sedona, these vortexes are said to amplify your energy, making it a hotspot for meditation, healing, and self-discovery. Some visitors report feeling a sense of calm and clarity, while others describe a physical sensation—a tingling in their hands or a warmth in their chest.

Sedona has four vortex sites: Cathedral Rock, Bell Rock, Airport Mesa, and Boynton Canyon. Each has its unique energy.

One tip is to go early in the morning or late in the afternoon. Not only will you avoid the crowds, but the changing light creates a magical atmosphere, with the red rocks glowing as if lit from within.

To explore these sites more deeply, consider joining a guided vortex tour. Many local guides are knowledgeable about their history, geology, and spiritual significance. Some tours even incorporate meditation or yoga, enriching the experience.

## Cathedral Rock and Bell Rock Hikes

If Sedona had a crown, Cathedral Rock and Bell Rock would be its jewels. Their stunning beauty and accessible trails make them a must-visit for any Sedona adventurer.

Let's start with Cathedral Rock, one of Sedona's most famous formations. The trail to Cathedral Rock is short but steep, a 1.2-mile round trip that rewards you with jaw-dropping views. As you climb, you'll navigate red rock ledges and scramble over boulders, each step bringing you closer to the breathtaking summit. The energy here is palpable—this is one of Sedona's main vortex sites, and many hikers pause at the top to meditate or soak in the serenity.

Next, let's discuss Bell Rock. Located just south of Sedona. It is another vortex site and a popular hiking destination. Unlike Cathedral Rock, Bell Rock offers a variety of trails, ranging from strolls to challenging climbs.

A great trail is the Bell Rock Pathway, a 3.6-mile round trip that loops around the base of the rock. The views are spectacular, with Bell Rock towering above and Courthouse Butte nearby. Though the ascent can be tricky, you can scramble up Bell Rock for the more adventurous.

## The Best Scenic Drives Around Sedona

Driving through Sedona is like stepping into a painting. The red rock formations rise dramatically against the blue sky. Whether you're a seasoned road-tripper or just looking for a leisurely drive, Sedona's scenic routes are guaranteed to take your breath away.

One of the most famous drives is the Red Rock Scenic Byway, Highway 179. This 7.5-mile stretch of road is often called a "museum without walls," and it's easy to see why. As you wind through the valley, you'll pass landmarks like Bell Rock, Cathedral Rock, and the Chapel of the Holy Cross. Plenty of pullouts are along the way, so take your time and stop to soak in the views.

Another must-drive route is Oak Creek Canyon, often called the smaller cousin of the Grand Canyon. The 14-mile stretch of Highway 89A between Sedona and Flagstaff is a beautiful drive. You'll wind through a lush canyon, with towering cliffs on either side and the sound of Oak Creek flowing below.

If you're feeling adventurous, consider exploring Schnebly Hill Road. This rugged, unpaved road takes you high into the mountains, offering panoramic views of Sedona and the surrounding wilderness. I'll warn you, though—it's not for the faint of heart. A high-clearance vehicle is a must, and the road can be rough.

## Sedona's Art and Cultural Scene

One of the best places to explore Sedona's art scene is the Tlaquepaque Arts and Crafts Village. This Mexican-style village is home to galleries, shops, and studios that showcase everything from fine art to handmade jewelry. Strolling through Tlaquepaque is like walking through an artist's dream.

Visit the Sedona Heritage Museum, which is housed in a homestead. The museum offers a glimpse into the lives of Sedona's early settlers.

Sedona is also known for its festivals, including the Sedona International Film Festival and the Sedona Arts Festival. These events bring together artists, filmmakers, and creatives from around the globe, making Sedona a cultural hotspot.

## Sedona and Red Rock Bucketlist

### 1. Amitabha Stupa and Peace Park

Nestled in Sedona's rugged terrain, the Amitabha Stupa and Peace Park are serene destinations for meditation, reflection, and renewal.

### 2. Red Rock Secret Mountain Wilderness

It offers a network of scenic canyons, cliffs, and mesas, offering trails less traveled and an unmatched sense of isolation.

### 3. Fay Canyon Arch Trail

Fay Canyon Arch Trail is a quieter gem. The short trail leads to a secret arch tucked away in the canyon.

### 4. Red Rock Crossing/ Crescent Moon Ranch

The crossing offers iconic views of Cathedral Rock reflected in the water; venture beyond to find quieter spots perfect for picnicking, journaling, or simply enjoying the sound of Oak Creek flowing by.

### 5. Seven Sacred Pools

Tucked along the Soldier Pass trail, the Seven Sacred Pools are a series of natural rock pools with spiritual allure.

### 6. Boynton Canyon's Enchantment Vortex

Sedona is known for its energy vortexes, and Boynton Canyon is one of the most accessible yet tranquil spots to feel the energy. Look out for Kachina Woman rock formation—it's said to be the source of the vortex's energy.

# CHAPTER 3

## Phoenix and the Valley of the Sun

---

*"Phoenix is not just a city; it's a desert oasis that rises, shines, and surprises with every visit."*

---

**Phoenix, Arizona, is a city that pulses with energy, sun, and a rich blend of history and modernity. Nestled in the Valley of the Sun, Phoenix serves as both Arizona's capital and the American Southwest's heartbeat.**

When you think of Phoenix, images of vast desert landscapes, towering cacti, and scorching sunshine may come to mind. But what you might not know is that this desert city is brimming with culture, outdoor adventure, and an eclectic food scene.

## Exploring Downtown Phoenix and Its Museums

Downtown Phoenix dynamically blends the old and the new with historic landmarks alongside modern architectural wonders. The area is filled with life, from its lively streets to its impressive arts and culture scene. Whether you're a history buff, an art lover, or simply someone who enjoys exploring a city's beating heart, downtown Phoenix will not disappoint.

One of the first places to visit is the Heard Museum. This museum focuses on Native American culture, history, craftsmanship, and traditions. Its exhibits are thought-provoking and beautifully curated.

And the Phoenix Art Museum should also be high on your list. It's the largest art museum in the southwestern United States, and walking through its halls is like embarking on a global art tour. You'll find works spanning centuries and continents, including European masterpieces, contemporary art, and diverse exhibitions that reflect the region's cultural richness.

Another standout spot in downtown is Roosevelt Row, a trendy district filled with art galleries, independent shops, and murals that create a colorful, almost bohemian atmosphere.

## Hiking in South Mountain Park

South Mountain Park is one of the largest municipal parks. It is expansive, with more than 16,000 acres of desert terrain, and offers an extensive network of hiking and biking trails, from easy strolls to more challenging summit hikes.

A favorite trail is the Holbert Trail, which leads to the top of a mountain saddle and offers panoramic views of the valley below.

Another popular trail is the National Trail, a longer, more strenuous route that takes you deep into the park's natural beauty. Along the way, you'll encounter desert flora, including saguaro cacti, creosote bushes, and palo verde trees.

South Mountain Park is not only about hiking, though—it's a great place to explore the region's unique desert environment. The park is home to Native American petroglyphs, remnants of ancient rock art created by the Hohokam people. These petroglyphs are scattered throughout the park, showing the area's history and culture.

The Dobbins Lookout offers a breathtaking view of the valley.

## Day Trips Around Phoenix

There's no shortage of day trip options that allow you to explore Arizona's natural wonders and hidden gems.

The Desert Botanical Garden. Located just outside the city, this 140-acre sanctuary for desert plants. The garden's trails lead through various ecosystems, showcasing the diversity of the desert's plant life.

For something a little different, consider taking a day trip to the nearby town of Jerome. Once a thriving copper mining town, Jerome is now a quirky, artsy destination perched on the side of a mountain. The town offers stunning views of the Verde Valley and is home to galleries, shops, and a fascinating history museum. Jerome is also known for its ghost tours—if you're into the supernatural, this town is said to be one of the most haunted places in Arizona.

Another great day trip option is to head north to Sedona. Just a two-hour drive from Phoenix, Sedona offers spectacular red rock formations, hiking trails, and vortex sites that attract visitors worldwide. The drive is beautiful, taking you through the high desert landscape and into the heart of Arizona's geological wonderland. Once you're in Sedona, you'll find plenty of hiking, art galleries, and spiritual experiences that are unique to this area.

For a more historical experience, visit the charming town of Prescott. Prescott offers a glimpse into Arizona's past with its Victorian-style buildings and historic courthouse. It also offers several outdoor activities, including hiking, fishing, and boating on Watson Lake.

## Phoenix & Valley of the Sun Bucketlist

### 1. Mystery Castle

Mystery Castle, built in the 1930s by a father for his daughter, is a labor of love etched into Phoenix. It is made from found and reused materials and finds beauty in the discarded.

### 2. Tovrea Castle at Carraro Heights

Tovrea Castle is a true hidden gem, part historic site, part architectural marvel. Though reservations are necessary, your patience will be rewarded with unforgettable views.

### 3. South Mountain's Petroglyphs (Hidden Rock Art)

These petroglyphs—created by the Hohokam people hundreds of years ago—remind us of those who thrived here under the same sun, facing challenges with equal resilience.

### 4. The Farm at South Mountain

Escape the urban rush at this serene oasis in the heart of Phoenix. With sprawling pecan trees and garden-to-table dining, it's the perfect place to slow down, reflect, and recharge.

### 5. Hole-in-the-Rock Formation

While often overshadowed by the more popular Papago Park, Hole-in-the-Rock offers a quieter, elevated view of the city where you can reflect on your journey.

### 6. Arizona Falls

Constructed in a tiny rivulet connecting neighborhoods, Arizona Falls presents an urban twist on nature. This hydro-powered art installation is equally functional as it is artistic.

# CHAPTER 4

## Grand Canyon's North Rim and Beyond

---

*"It's not the mountain we conquer, but ourselves." – Sir Edmund Hillary*

---

**The Grand Canyon's North Rim is less crowded and more rugged than its Southern counterpart, the North Rim offers a different perspective on this natural wonder.**

The North Rim boasts over 1,000 feet of additional elevation compared to the South Rim, which means cooler temperatures and lush forests of aspen and pine. A favorite trail on this side of the canyon is the Widforss Trail.

Another trail you can't miss is the North Kaibab Trail. This one is unique because it's the only trail that takes you below the rim on this side of the canyon. Even a short trek to the Coconino Overlook gives you an unforgettable glimpse of the canyon's grandeur.

And the Ken Patrick Trail is a ticket to peace. It's not uncommon to go hours without encountering another hiker.

## Discovering the Remote Beauty of Cape Royal

Cape Royal can steal your breath and make you feel like you've stepped into a postcard. The panoramic views here are unmatched, with the Colorado River snaking its way through the canyon.

One of the highlights of Cape Royal is the Angel's Window, a natural arch that frames the canyon beyond it.

## Scenic Drives Through Kaibab National Forest

The journey through the Kaibab National Forest is nothing short of magical. It is one of the few places to experience such dramatic contrasts in a short distance.

The Forest Service Road 22 is a must-drive route. This gravel road takes us deep into the forest, where towering ponderosa pines stretch toward the sky. Keep your eyes peeled—you might spot deer, wild turkeys, or even the elusive Kaibab squirrel, a species found only in this part of the world.

Another scenic drive you'll love is the Point Imperial Road. This paved route leads to the highest viewpoint on the North Rim, Point Imperial. From this vantage point, you can see the Painted Desert in the distance and the winding curves of the Colorado River far below. And because this area is less visited than other parts of the Grand Canyon, you often have the road to yourself.

## Grand Canyon's North Rim Bucketlist

### 1. Cape Final Hike

Cape Final Trail is a peaceful 4-mile round-trip hike through pine forests that offers panoramic canyon views.

### 2. Point Imperial

At 8,803 feet, Point Imperial is the highest viewpoint in the Grand Canyon. This is where the Vermilion Cliffs first meet the canyon.

### 3. Roaring Springs

Roaring Springs along the North Kaibab Trail is unforgettable. Woven through towering cliffs and lush pockets of greenery, the trail mirrors life itself—challenging, beautiful, but worth every step.

### 4. Angel's Window

Angel's Window is a natural rock formation near the Cape Royal Trail, delivering a stunning view of the Colorado River.

### 5. Torry Weeping Rock

Torry Weeping Rock is named for the streams of water that "weep" from the stone, creating a mesmerizing and meditative atmosphere.

### 6. Walhalla Glades and Ruins

Visit the ancient Puebloan ruins at Walhalla Glades. These dwellings tell the story of a people deeply connected to the land.

### 7. Bright Angel Point

Bright Angel Point remains a must-see for its 360-degree views of the canyon and the surrounding Kaibab Plateau.

# CHAPTER 5

# Tucson and the Sonoran Desert

---

***"The desert tells a different story every time one ventures on it." – Robert Edison Fulton Jr.***

---

**Tucson is nestled in the heart of the Sonoran Desert, this vibrant city is surrounded by towering saguaro cacti, rugged mountains, and a unique blend of cultures that make it unlike anywhere else in the world.**

Let's kick things off with one of Tucson's crown jewels: Saguaro National Park. This park is split into two districts—east and west—flanking the city like a pair of protective arms. If you've never seen a saguaro cactus, prepare to be amazed. These towering giants are the iconic symbols of the American Southwest.

The Tucson Mountain District is home to some of the densest saguaro forests you'll ever see. The Valley View Overlook Trail is a great introduction. It's a relatively short hike, but it offers sweeping views of the desert floor dotted with saguaros as far as the eye can see.

For a more immersive experience, the Signal Hill Trail is a must. This easy hike leads to a hilltop adorned with ancient petroglyphs. Imagine standing in the same spot where indigenous peoples etched their stories into the rocks centuries ago. Moments like these make Saguaro National Park so special—it's not just a place of natural beauty but a living testament to history.

Rincon Mountain District has higher elevations and more diverse vegetation, including oak and pine forests. The Cactus Forest Drive is a scenic loop that takes you through some of the park's most picturesque parts.

The Douglas Spring Trail offers an unforgettable journey into the Rincon Mountains, with seasonal waterfalls and breathtaking vistas.

Saguaro National Park is also a fantastic place for night adventures. The desert sky comes alive after dark; stargazing here is second to none.

## Tucson's History and Culture

Tucson's rich history and vibrant culture are woven into every city corner. You'll find a blend of Spanish, Mexican, and Native American influences that give Tucson its unique character.

Starting at Mission San Xavier del Bac, often called the "White Dove of the Desert," this 18th-century Spanish mission is a masterpiece of Baroque architecture. Its gleaming white exterior against the blue desert sky is a sight. As you step inside, you'll be greeted by intricate frescoes, ornate carvings, and a profound sense of tranquility.

Then head to El Presidio Historic District, the heart of Tucson's Old Town. As you wander its narrow streets, you'll feel like you've returned in time. Some of the adobe buildings date back to the 19th century. Stop by the Tucson Museum of Art, which showcases an impressive collection of Southwestern art, from pre-Columbian artifacts to contemporary works.

Tucson has a thriving food scene deeply rooted in its cultural heritage. El Charro Café is the oldest Mexican restaurant in the U.S.; the same family still operates there. Their carne seca, a dried beef dish made using traditional methods, is a must-try.

For a modern twist, visit Tucson Tamale Company and sample tamales with fillings like green chile pork or black beans.

## Hiking Mount Lemmon and the Catalina Mountains

Next, visit Mount Lemmon, the crown jewel of the Catalina Mountains. Rising over 9,000 feet above sea level, this mountain offers a refreshing escape from Tucson's scorching temperatures.

A favorite trail here is the Marshall Gulch Trail, a shaded path that winds through pine forests and alongside babbling brooks. The air here is cool and crisp, starkly contrasting to the desert below. You'll pass wildflowers, towering trees, and the occasional rock formation that begs to be climbed. The trail connects to the Aspen Trail, creating a loop that offers stunning views of the surrounding mountains.

The Lemmon Rock Lookout Trail is a must if you're up for a challenge. This steep, strenuous hike rewards you with panoramic views from the summit. On a clear day, you can see Mexico.

For those who prefer a more relaxed adventure, the SkyCenter Observatory offers guided nighttime stargazing programs. Mount Lemmon's high altitude and clear skies make it ideal for stargazing.

## Exploring the Arizona-Sonora Desert Museum

The Arizona-Sonora Desert Museum is part zoo, part botanical garden, and part natural history exhibit—all rolled into one incredible experience. If you want to understand the beauty and complexity of the Sonoran Desert truly, this is the place to start.

Walking through the museum's outdoor exhibits, you'll encounter a stunning array of desert plants and animals. In the Riparian Corridor, you can see beavers, otters, and even a mountain lion in a recreated desert stream environment.

The Raptor Free Flight Program is another highlight. Watching these magnificent birds soar above you, responding to the calls of their trainers, is nothing short of magical. It's rare to see hawks, falcons, and owls up close and learn about their role in the desert.

The museum also features an extensive cactus garden, showcasing everything from tiny barrel cacti to towering saguaros. You'll be amazed by the variety of shapes, sizes, and colors.

For an educational experience, the museum's geology exhibit offers fascinating insights into the forces that shaped the Sonoran Desert. You can touch ancient rock formations, explore a recreated cave, and learn about the region's mining history.

## Tucson and the Sonoran Desert Bucketlist

### 1. Saguaro National Park's Secret Trails

Skip the main tourist paths and hike the Valley View Overlook Trail or Wasson Peak via Hugh Norris Trail.

**2. Madera Canyon**

Nestled just south of Tucson, Madera Canyon is a lush oasis perfect for a change of pace. It is known for its incredible birdwatching (you might spot a rare Elegant Trogon!).

**3. Mission San Xavier del Bac**

This "White Dove of the Desert" is an 18th-century Spanish mission and serves as an architectural masterpiece and spiritual retreat.

**4. Sabino Canyon's Hidden Pools**

While Sabino Canyon is well-trodden, its hidden pools offer a different experience if you want to seek them out. Ride the tram and hop off at stop 9, then hike up to Seven Falls Trail for an unforgettable encounter with water in the desert.

**5. Tumamoc Hill**

If you're up for an early morning challenge, hike Tumamoc Hill as the sun crests the horizon.

**6. Ironwood Forest National Monument**

The Ironwood Forest National Monument has ancient trees, rugged mountains, and endless skies.

**7. Colossal Cave Mountain Park**

Escape the heat and enter the world of Colossal Cave, a hidden labyrinth of tunnels and chambers just outside Tucson.

### 8. The Sonoran Desert's Night Sky

Kitt Peak National Observatory or even remote desert camping spots allow you to wonder at the infinite universe above.

### 9. Barrio Viejo's Colorful Streets

The historic Barrio Viejo neighborhood has vibrant adobe houses, and quiet streets take you back in time.

### 10. Inspiring Desert Art at DeGrazia Gallery in the Sun

Tucked into the foothills of Tucson, this gallery built by artist Ettore "Ted" DeGrazia blends beautifully into the surrounding desert.

# CHAPTER 6

## The Wonders of Page

---

*"There is no greater beauty in the world than what we see in the places that we've never before." – Anonymous*

---

**Nestled between the red rock formations of the Arizona-Utah border lies adventurers and nature lovers alike—Lake Powell. This reservoir stretches over 180 miles and offers stunning vistas, crystal-clear waters, world-renowned natural landmarks, and adrenaline-pumping outdoor activities.**

## Exploring the Glen Canyon Dam and Antelope Canyon

Page is the Glen Canyon Dam, a marvel of engineering that has shaped the landscape of Lake Powell. Built in the 1960s, the dam's impressive concrete walls rise 710 feet above the Colorado River. The dam offers spectacular views and the chance to understand the area's history and significance.

Antelope Canyon is one of the world's most photographed and iconic slot canyons. The narrow passageways of Antelope Canyon are carved into the Navajo Sandstone.

Antelope Canyon has two parts: Upper Antelope Canyon and Lower Antelope Canyon. Both are equally stunning, but they offer different experiences. Upper Antelope Canyon is more popular for photography and a more leisurely hike.

Lower Antelope Canyon is a bit more adventurous. The narrow pathways and stairs make it more physically demanding, but the views are equally spectacular.

## Hiking in Horseshoe Bend

The Horseshoe Bend Trail is about a mile round-trip. The trail is well-marked and takes you across a sandy path to the cliff's edge, where you'll be greeted with the awe-inspiring view of the river curving through the canyon below.

Several nearby trails offer great perspectives of the Colorado River and surrounding rock formations. The Kayenta Trail is a longer, more strenuous hike that leads to more stunning canyon views.

## Hidden Gems Around Page

Page might be small, but it's surrounded by some of the most jaw-dropping landscapes in the Southwest and is packed with hidden gems waiting to be explored.

The Wave is a stunning sandstone in the Paria Canyon-Vermilion Cliffs Wilderness. It's a tough hike to reach, and you need a permit to access it, but the reward is worth it.

Waterholes Canyon is located outside of Page. This slot canyon is less crowded than Antelope Canyon, yet it's just as mesmerizing. Waterholes Canyon is the perfect place for a more serene and personal adventure.

Head to Castle Rock, which offers incredible views from many parts of Lake Powell. You can reach the base by boat, or if you're feeling adventurous, you can hike up the rocky slopes to capture panoramic shots of the lake and the surrounding cliffs.

## Lake Powell and Page Bucketlist

### 1. Alcove Canyon

Quiet, secluded, and utterly enchanting, Alcove Canyon is often overshadowed by its more famous sibling, Antelope Canyon.

### 2. Hanging Garden Trail

This lesser-known trail near Page leads to a marvelous desert oasis: The Hanging Garden. It is a lush surprise in an arid landscape.

### 3. Stud Horse Point

Stud Horse Point is a unique spot of hoodoo rock formations.

### 4. Navajo Canyon

Navajo Canyon offers a different kind of magic. Paddle your way through its winding path, surrounded by towering cliffs.

### 5. Lone Rock Beach Stargazing

The shorelines of Lone Rock Beach offer a play of contrasts—soft sand underfoot while colossal sandstone towers above you.

### 6. Antelope Point's Floating Walkways (Off Peak)

Antelope Point Marina during off-peak hours. The floating walkways offer a serene stroll, surrounded by the calm of Lake Powell's water.

**7. Waterholes Canyon**

Waterholes Canyon offers beauty—without the crowds.

**8. The Chains**

The Chains is a secluded area near Glen Canyon Dam, where smooth sandstone meets the shimmering waters of Lake Powell.

# CHAPTER 7

# Arizona's Native American Heritage and Cultural Sites

---

***"To understand the true heart of a land, you must first understand the people who have lived in it for centuries." – Anonymous***

---

**As you explore the vast landscapes of Arizona, you'll quickly discover that the land is more than just a canvas of desert plains, red rocks, and towering cacti.**

Arizona is home to two of the most prominent Native American tribes in the United States: the Hopi and the Navajo. Both tribes have deep-rooted traditions that go back centuries, and visiting their reservations offers a rare opportunity to learn firsthand about their cultures, art, and way of life.

The Hopi Reservation in northeastern Arizona is one of the oldest continuously inhabited places in the United States. The Hopi people are known for their deep spiritual connection to the land and remarkable ability to live harmoniously with nature. They are famous for their intricate Kachina dolls, pottery, and weaving, all of which hold profound cultural significance.

When you visit the Hopi Reservation, you'll have the chance to explore the Hopi Villages, some of which have been perched atop mesas for over a thousand years.

One of the most important experiences on the Hopi Reservation is visiting the Hopi Cultural Center, where you can learn about the tribe's history, rituals, and art. The center also has a museum and gift shop where you can purchase authentic Hopi crafts, which help support the local community. If you time your visit right, you may even have the chance to witness a traditional Hopi dance ceremony or other sacred events that connect the Hopi people to their ancestors.

The Navajo Nation, covering over 27,000 square miles across northeastern Arizona, is the largest Native American reservation in the United States. The Navajo people are renowned for their rich cultural heritage, which includes weaving, jewelry-making, and traditional rug-making.

One of the highlights of a visit to the Navajo Reservation is the opportunity to tour Monument Valley Navajo Tribal Park, which features iconic sandstone formations rising from the desert floor.

You can take a guided tour with a Navajo guide who will share insights into the land's history, culture, and spiritual significance.

Another must-see is the Navajo Code Talkers Museum in Window Rock, the capital of the Navajo Nation. It honors the Navajo soldiers who played a crucial role in World War II by using their language to create an unbreakable code for military communications.

## The Petrified Forest and Painted Desert

As you travel through northeastern Arizona, the Petrified Forest and the Painted Desert are testaments to the power of nature and time. Both are geological wonders with rich cultural history embedded in their rock layers.

Together, these two landscapes create one of Arizona's most visually striking places. They offer visitors a chance to explore ancient natural history and the cultural heritage of the Native peoples who have lived there for centuries.

The Petrified Forest National Park is a mesmerizing landscape filled with colorful, fossilized trees that date back over 200 million years. Once part of a lush forest, these ancient trees were buried by volcanic ash and preserved as petrified wood. As you walk through the park, you'll see logs that have turned into stone, their vibrant colors ranging from shades of red and orange to purple and green.

The park has several well-marked trails, and the Blue Mesa trail is particularly striking. The petrified wood's blue and purple hues contrast beautifully with the desert's red soil and skies.

Adjacent to the Petrified Forest is the Painted Desert, a stretch of land known for its stunning array of colors. The desert's mesas, buttes, and cliffs are painted red, orange, pink, and purple.

One of the best ways to experience the Painted Desert is to drive along the Painted Desert Rim Drive. You'll stop at various overlooks and trails, each offering a unique perspective of the desert's beauty. The Painted Desert has long been significant to Native American cultures. The landscape is woven into the creation myths of the Navajo and Hopi peoples.

## The Heard Museum

Visit the Heard Museum in Phoenix to delve deeper into Arizona's Native American heritage. The museum is one of the most comprehensive and respected institutions for preserving and showcasing Native American art and culture.

The Heard Museum boasts an impressive collection of Native American art, from traditional to contemporary. Its intricate silver jewelry, pottery, textiles, and basketry represent different tribes and artistic traditions.

One of the museum's highlights is its American Indian Hall, which houses an extensive collection of historic objects, including clothing, tools, and ceremonial items, that tell the story of Native American life before European contact.

## Exploring the Ruins of Canyon de Chelly

Finally, no journey through Arizona's Native American heritage would be complete without a visit to the ruins of Canyon de Chelly. Located in northeastern Arizona, Canyon de Chelly is one of the most well-preserved archaeological sites and one of the most spiritually significant places for the Navajo people.

The canyon is home to several ancient Ancestral Puebloan ruins, including cliff dwellings dating back to around 350 AD. The most famous is the White House Ruin, which offers a stunning view of the well-preserved dwellings in the canyon's walls. Many ruins are still sacred to the Navajo people.

Canyon de Chelly National Monument is located within the Navajo Nation. It is a place where history, culture, and natural beauty come together in a truly unforgettable way.

## Native American Heritage Bucketlist

### 1. Hopi Mesas

The Hopi Mesas provide an authentic glimpse into one of North America's oldest continuously inhabited communities. These villages, perched on mesas for over 1,000 years, tell the story of the Hopi people and their deeply spiritual way of life.

**2. Montezuma Castle**

This well-preserved cliff dwelling was once home to the Sinagua people. Marvel at how these ancient engineers built homes within cliffs to survive the desert's challenges.

**3. Navajo National Monument**

The Navajo National Monument features the incredible Betatakin and Keet Seel cliff dwellings. These sites showcase the craftsmanship of the Ancestral Puebloans.

**4. Hubbell Trading Post National Historic Site**

The Hubbell Trading Post is a living piece of history that continues to serve as a crossroads for culture and trade.

**5. Painted Rock Petroglyph Site**

The Painted Rock Petroglyph Site is a treasure of ancient rock art.

**6. Walnut Canyon National Monument**

Walnut Canyon features cliff dwellings nestled into the canyon walls. The Sinagua people once called this place home, and walking the Island Trail will lead you right into their world.

### 7. Tuzigoot National Monument

Set against the Verde River Valley, Tuzigoot showcases the remains of a hilltop pueblo built by the Sinagua people.

### 8. The White Mountains - Apache Lands

The White Mountains showcase the diversity of Apache lands.

# CHAPTER 8

## Historic Route 66 and the Old West

***"The great American road trip is about exploring the spirit of freedom, and no highway better embodies that spirit than Route 66."***

**Route 66 is not just a road; it's a legend, an iconic symbol of the American journey. In Arizona, the road cuts through some of the country's most captivating landscapes and historical sites.**

Route 66 is known as "The Main Street of America," and it's easy to see why. This historic highway, which once spanned nearly 2,500 miles from Chicago to Santa Monica, is known for its charming towns, quirky roadside attractions, and scenic vistas it offers.

## Visiting Seligman, Williams, and Kingman

Seligman is a small town that's become one of the most celebrated stops along Route 66. Nestled in the high desert, Seligman is like a time capsule, capturing the essence of the 1950s and 1960s roadside Americana.

There's something magical about Seligman's preservation of its Route 66 heritage. Many buildings still feature the original signs, offering an authentic look at life for travelers during the highway's heyday.

One of the must-see stops in Seligman is the Snow Cap Drive-In, a quirky diner that's practically a legend. Established in the 1950s, the Snow Cap has become known for its colorful decor, playful atmosphere, and delicious burgers.

Next, Williams awaits you—a town that prides itself on being "The Gateway to the Grand Canyon." The city has preserved much of its historic charm, from the old-fashioned railroads to the historic hotels and motels lining the street. Williams is the place to experience a blend of Old West history and Route 66 nostalgia, with attractions like the Grand Canyon Railway. Williams hosts the annual "Route 66 Festival," a celebration of the highway's legacy, where visitors can enjoy classic cars, live music, and more.

Finally, Kingman is lined with motels, gas stations, and diners that evoke the golden age of road trips. The Mohave Museum of History and Arts is also worth a visit, offering exhibits on the region's history, including its role as a key stop on Route 66.

## Exploring Arizona's Mining Towns

As you continue your journey along Route 66, a detour through Arizona's mining towns is an absolute must. Two of the most fascinating towns you can visit are Jerome and Bisbee.

Jerome, once known as the "Wickedest Town in the West," sits on the side of Cleopatra Hill, offering jaw-dropping views of the surrounding Verde Valley. This former copper mining town flourished in the early 20th century but faced economic decline after the mines were depleted. Today, Jerome has reinvented itself as an artist enclave, with galleries, shops, and restaurants occupying historic buildings that once housed miners and their families.

The Jerome State Historic Park is an essential stop in town. It offers a fascinating look at the area's history. Located in the former mansion of the local mine manager, the park houses exhibits on the town's mining history and the people who lived and worked there.

A short drive from Jerome is Bisbee, another former mining town. Known for its Victorian architecture and artistic atmosphere, Bisbee has become a haven for artists, musicians, and history buffs alike. The town's history as a copper mining hub is still evident, and the Queen

Mine offers guided tours that take visitors deep into the earth to explore the tunnels where miners once worked.

Bisbee's preservation efforts have preserved much of its 19th-century charm, making it a great place to soak up the Old West ambiance. Visiting Bisbee is a chance to explore the past and present, as the town's rich history and artistic spirit blend seamlessly into modern-day culture.

## Arizona's Cowboy Heritage and Museums

Arizona's Wild West history is alive and well, with numerous museums and historical sites celebrating the state's legacy of cattle ranching, law enforcement officers, and outlaws.

One of the most iconic places to learn about Arizona's cowboy past is the Arizona Cowboy Hall of Fame in Phoenix. This museum is dedicated to preserving the legacy of the men and women who shaped the state's Western culture.

Scottsdale's Museum of the West showcases the history of the American West. Its exhibits highlight Native American culture, cowboy life, and Arizona's role in shaping the West. The museum's collection includes artifacts, art, and interactive displays.

Next, Tombstone is a must-visit. Famous for the gunfight at the O.K. Corral, Tombstone has preserved much of its historic charm with reenactments and museums that bring the Wild West to life. From walking the streets where legends like Wyatt Earp and Doc Holliday once roamed to visiting the famous Bird Cage Theatre, Tombstone is where the past and present collide thrillingly.

## Arizona Historic Route 66 Bucketlist

**1. Hackberry General Store** (Hackberry, AZ)

The Hackberry General Store is an old-fashioned roadside pit stop brimming with Route 66 memorabilia, classic cars, and local stories etched into every corner.

**2. Grand Canyon Caverns** (Peach Springs, AZ)

Venture 210 feet underground into a unique natural limestone cavern that doubles as a subterranean time capsule. Tours showcase artifacts from the 1920s and the Cold War era.

**3. Meteor Crater** (Winslow, AZ)

Meteor Crater, formed around 50,000 years ago, offers an incredible view of Earth's natural power. Visitors can walk along its edge or explore the on-site Discovery Center.

**4. Sycamore Falls** (Williams, AZ)

Sycamore Falls is tucked away in the Kaibab National Forest. Its cliffs and wilderness surround a seasonal cascade.

**5. Ash Fork's Route 66 Museum** (Ash Fork, AZ)

This small yet fascinating museum celebrates Route 66's legacy with quirky exhibits and a collection of vintage signs.

**6. Two Guns Ghost Town** (Near Winslow, AZ)

Among the ruins, you'll discover an old trading post and crumbling signs of a story etched into the Arizona desert's expanse.

**7. Painted Desert Trading Post** (Near Holbrook, AZ)

A long-abandoned trading post, this historic site sits along a now-defunct stretch of Route 66. It's a picturesque stop for Route 66 enthusiasts and photographers seeking an authentic slice of history.

**8. Hidden Petroglyph Sites Near Flagstaff**

Seek out sites like Picture Canyon or Keyhole Sink to marvel at artwork left by Native Americans centuries ago.

# CHAPTER 9

## Arizona's Best National and State Parks

*"The earth has music for those who listen." – George Santayana*

Arizona's national and state parks are the epitome of outdoor adventure, offering iconic natural wonders and hidden gems that captivate your spirit. With rugged deserts, vast canyons, towering pines, and ancient rock formations, these parks provide a landscape like no other.

## A Complete Guide to Grand Canyon National Park

As one of the most visited national parks in the world, the Grand Canyon National Park offers endless opportunities for exploration, from hikes along the rim to thrilling descents into the canyon's depths.

The Grand Canyon is not just a geological marvel; it's a historical and cultural treasure. The park spans over 277 miles and reaches depths of over a mile, offering a jaw-dropping view of the Earth's history written in the rock layers. But there's more to the canyon than meets the eye.

The Colorado River, which carved the canyon over millions of years, still flows through the park's heart, providing opportunities for whitewater rafting and river adventures.

The park's most popular area is the South Rim, which is easily accessible and home to the main visitor center. I recommend starting here, where you can enjoy breathtaking panoramic views and plan your exploration from several scenic overlooks.

The Bright Angel Trail and South Kaibab Trail are the most famous routes. The Bright Angel Trail, with its stunning views and manageable distance, is great for beginners. However, remember that hiking down into the canyon is one thing; hiking back up is another.

For those seeking a more relaxed experience, there are plenty of easy walks along the rim, such as the Rim Trail, which offers unobstructed views without the strenuous effort of descending into the canyon.

Alternatively, consider the Grand Canyon Railway, a vintage train ride from Williams to the park's South Rim on a scenic journey. The Grand Canyon also offers some unique experiences, including stargazing at night. As a designated International Dark Sky Park, the Grand Canyon is one of the best places in the country to see the stars.

## Visiting Petrified Forest National Park

Petrified Forest National Park is one of Arizona's hidden gems. It is a place where ancient history and striking natural beauty meet. The park is a world-renowned fossil site known for its colorful, millions-of-year-old petrified wood.

One of the best ways to experience the park is by taking a scenic drive along the park's main road, which passes by some of the most iconic features, including the Rainbow Forest and the Blue Mesa. As you wind your way through the park, you'll see the remarkable petrified logs, some of which are as large as trees and are brilliantly colored in shades of red, pink, purple, and yellow. These fossilized trees were once part of a lush forest long before the area became a desert. Over millions of years, the wood turned to stone, preserving the intricate patterns and textures of the original trees.

But Petrified Forest is more than just its petrified wood. The park also features ancient petroglyphs left by the Native American tribes that once lived in the region and a fascinating collection of historic Route 66 landmarks. The Painted Desert Inn, a historic building built in the

1930s, is a great stop to learn about the park's history and the cultures that shaped it. The inn now serves as a museum and a visitor center, where you can explore exhibits that bring the past to life.

The park offers several trails for hikers that allow you to get up close to the petrified wood and explore the area on foot. The Crystal Forest Trail is one of the park's most popular, providing a stroll among the colorful logs. If you're looking for something more challenging, the Blue Mesa Trail takes you down into a canyon, where the scenery is nothing short of otherworldly.

The Petrified Forest is also an excellent place for stargazing. It is located in a remote part of Arizona with little light pollution. During the summer, the park hosts evening programs where visitors can learn about the night sky and the constellations visible from this location.

## Exploring Slide Rock State Park and Oak Creek Canyon

Slide Rock State Park is the perfect blend of natural beauty and outdoor fun, especially if you want to cool off during the hot Arizona summers. Nestled in Oak Creek Canyon, this park offers one of the most unique swimming experiences in the state. The park's namesake is Slide Rock, a natural water slide created by smooth, red rock that allows you to slide down into the crystal-clear creek below.

The park is beside Sedona, a town famous for its striking red rock formations and vibrant arts scene. As you drive into the park, you'll be struck by the beauty of Oak Creek Canyon, a lush and narrow canyon surrounded by towering cliffs. The canyon is a haven for hikers, with several trails that offer views of the creek, waterfalls, and surrounding forests.

The Slide Rock area is great for families, as the water is shallow enough for children to play safely, while the surrounding rocks provide plenty of spots to relax and soak in the scenery.

The natural water slide is the main attraction, and it's easy to see why. The smooth, sloping rocks form a slippery slide that sends you careening into the cool water below, providing a refreshing and exhilarating experience. The park also features several other swimming holes where you can dip or simply relax by the water.

Aside from swimming, the park offers a range of activities, including hiking, picnicking, and wildlife watching. Oak Creek Canyon is home to various species of birds and other wildlife, making it a great spot for nature enthusiasts. The area is also known for its apple orchards, and in the fall, you can visit the park for apple picking, making it a perfect seasonal destination.

## Arizona National and State Parks Bucketlist

### 1. Picacho Peak State Park

Located between Phoenix and Tucson, this lesser-known park offers jaw-dropping desert views and a challenging trek. The Hunter Trail leads you to the summit of Picacho Peak.

**2. Chiricahua National Monument – Discover "A Wonderland of Rocks"**

Chiricahua National Monument is a geological wonderland with towering rock formations that look like sculptures carved by the hands of time.

**3. Tonto Natural Bridge State Park**

A bit off the beaten path, this park features a natural travertine bridge that spans 400 feet. Spend time hiking beneath this natural marvel or cooling off by the creek below.

**4. Havasu Falls**

Few venture deep into the Grand Canyon to experience the electric-blue beauty of Havasu Falls and Creek.

**5. Saguaro National Park**

Split into East and West districts bracketing Tucson, Saguaro National Park is a sanctuary for the iconic saguaro cacti. Wander through the Cactus Forest Trail or admire a fiery sunset over the desert.

**6. Alamo Canyon at Organ Pipe Cactus National Monument**

This remote corner of the Sonoran Desert offers a quiet refuge for those seeking solitude and a hike through Alamo Canyon's rugged trails.

**7. Kartchner Caverns State Park**

Kartchner Caverns offers guided tours through living caves filled with stalactites and stalagmites.

**8. Homolovi State Park**

For those drawn to history and spirituality, Homolovi State Park near Winslow preserves the ruins of ancient Hopi villages.

**9. Coal Mine Canyon**

This hidden gem in the Navajo Nation is a jaw-dropping mix of vibrant colors and dramatic cliffs.

**10. Dead Horse Ranch State Park**

Located near Cottonwood, this park's serene lagoons and the Verde River are perfect for kayaking or paddleboarding.

**11. Lost Dutchman State Park**

Nestled in the Superstition Mountains, this park is steeped in legend. The hike to the Flatiron rewards you with an unmatched view of the sprawling desert.

**12. White Pocket**

White Pocket on the Vermilion Cliffs offers a surreal landscape of colorful swirls and waves etched into sandstone.

# CHAPTER 10

## Exploring the Arizona Tonto National Forest

---

*"The forest is the best playmate, the natural wonder that invites us into a world where adventure and serenity dance together." – Anonymous*

---

**Tonto National Forest is one of Arizona's crown jewels, an expansive and diverse wilderness that invites every type of adventurer. Stretching across nearly 3 million acres of pristine desert, riparian habitats, and rugged mountains, this national forest is a paradise for those seeking outdoor adventure.**

Tonto National Forest is a hiker's dream. With over 200 miles of trails, the forest offers some of Arizona's most scenic and diverse landscapes. The Saguaro Lake Trail offers panoramic views of Saguaro Lake and the surrounding desert landscape. The trailhead is located near the edge of the lake. As you hike along, you'll find yourself marveling at the vastness of the desert—wide-open spaces dotted with cacti, dry riverbeds, and occasional bursts of color from blooming wildflowers.

The Four Peaks Trail offers a much more challenging adventure. It leads to Four Peaks, one of the highest points in the forest. As you gain elevation, the landscape transforms from desert to ponderosa pine forests, and the air becomes cooler and fresher.

Another trail is the Peralta Trail near the Superstition Mountains. Known for its striking views of the Superstition Wilderness, this trail is one of the most popular in the forest. You'll pass through diverse landscapes as you hike, including desert scrub and rocky outcrops. The trail ends at a viewpoint overlooking the Weaver's Needle, a towering rock formation that stands as a sentinel over the wilderness.

The Tonto Creek Trail is a hidden gem. This trail follows the creek, where the sound of flowing water and the shade of tall cottonwoods create a peaceful atmosphere. The trail is relatively easy, with minimal elevation gain, making it perfect for a relaxing day hike. Along the way, you may spot wildlife, such as deer or birds.

## Exploring Apache Lake and Roosevelt Lake

Apache Lake and Roosevelt Lake are among the most tranquil spots in Tonto National Forest. Nestled between rugged mountains and desert expanses, these lakes offer a refreshing escape from the heat and the perfect opportunity to connect with the water.

Apache Lake is the smaller of the two, but it's no less impressive. The lake is located along the Apache Trail, a historic route traversing the forest's eastern part.

The lake is somewhat remote, making it an excellent spot for those seeking a more peaceful experience away from the crowds. Boating, fishing, and kayaking are all popular activities here, and there's a certain tranquility that comes with spending a day on the water surrounded by mountains and deserts.

Apache Lake offers some excellent fishing opportunities. The lake is stocked with various fish species, including bass and catfish, and the surrounding area provides plenty of access points for boaters and shore fishermen.

Roosevelt Lake is the largest of the two lakes and one of the most popular spots in Tonto National Forest. It is located just off the Beeline Highway and offers plenty of recreational opportunities, including boating, fishing, and watersports.

One of the highlights of Roosevelt Lake is the Roosevelt Lake Bridge, which spans the lake and offers some breathtaking views of the surrounding area. The bridge is particularly striking at sunset.

For those who enjoy boating, Roosevelt Lake offers ample space to explore, whether in a kayak, a canoe, or a motorized boat. The lake's many coves and inlets provide plenty of opportunities to find a quiet spot to relax, swim, or picnic. You can also rent a boat and spend the day exploring the lake or try your hand at water skiing or wakeboarding.

## Camping and Boating in Tonto National Forest

Camping and boating are two of the most popular activities in Tonto National Forest, and for good reason. The forest's vast landscape is dotted with countless campgrounds and secluded spots to set up camp and enjoy the great outdoors.

Some of the most popular campgrounds in Tonto include Blue Point Campground, located near Roosevelt Lake, and Tonto Creek Campground, nestled in the cool pine forests near the Mogollon Rim. These developed campgrounds offer amenities like picnic tables, fire rings, and restrooms, making them perfect for families and beginners. For a more rustic experience, visit Fool Hollow Lake Recreation Area near Show Low.

Boating in Tonto National Forest is equally enjoyable, with several lakes offering opportunities for motorized boating, kayaking, canoeing, and paddleboarding. Roosevelt Lake is the largest and most well-known spot for boating in the forest, but other lakes are equally beautiful and less crowded, such as Bartlett Lake and Horseshoe Reservoir.

Whether you're kayaking along the shores of Saguaro Lake, cruising across the sparkling waters of Roosevelt Lake, or fishing from a boat on Apache Lake, the water activities in Tonto are nothing short of exhilarating.

Tonto National Forest also offers several backcountry camping opportunities to escape it all and experience the wilderness in its rawest form. These primitive campsites require more preparation and a willingness to disconnect from modern amenities. Remember to follow Leave No Trace principles and pack everything you bring in.

## Wildlife Watching in the Tonto Wilderness

Wildlife watching in Tonto National Forest is an incredible experience. The forest is home to many animals, from desert-dwelling reptiles to majestic birds of prey and elusive mammals. It offers a range of habitats, from desert and riparian areas to pine forests and rugged mountains, each attracting different wildlife species.

The desert bighorn sheep is one of the most iconic animals you'll encounter in Tonto. These impressive creatures are well adapted to the harsh desert environment, and spotting them on the cliffs and hillsides is always a thrill.

Tonto is also home to various bird species, making it a fantastic destination for birdwatching. The forest's diverse ecosystems attract everything from soaring eagles and red-tailed hawks to migratory songbirds and waterfowl. If you're a bird enthusiast, Tonto National Forest offers countless opportunities to spot these fascinating creatures in their natural habitats.

## Tonto National Forest Bucketlist

### 1. Fossil Creek

Fossil Creek is a sanctuary of turquoise waterfalls, crystal-clear swimming holes, and lush vegetation.

### 2. The Wave Cave

This wave-shaped rock formation, hidden in the Superstition Wilderness, is perfect for adventurers ready for a short, steep hike.

### 3. Seven Springs Recreation Area

Seven Springs is an off-the-radar haven surrounded by lush riparian vegetation, boasting a refreshing creek, vibrant wildflowers (in season), and scenic walking trails.

### 4. The Ellison Creek Cascades

This hidden waterfall rewards those willing to explore beyond the usual tourist trails. Perfect for a summer hike, the pools here invite you to cool off and breathe in the forest's peace.

**5. Four Peaks Wilderness Area**

Four Peaks Wilderness itself is a unique experience. With trails ranging from moderate to challenging, this area rewards hikers with sweeping views of the desert and lakes.

**6. Haigler Creek**

Nestled near the Mogollon Rim, Haigler Creek feels like a well-kept secret. It's a destination for fishing, wading, or simply nature.

**7. Devil's Canyon**

Devil's Canyon offers a genuinely remote adventure. This hidden gem in the eastern portion of Tonto is ideal for those craving solitude and awe-inspiring rock formations.

**8. Box Canyon (near Wickenburg)**

Waterfalls, winding canyons, and a landscape that will take your breath away—Box Canyon is a delight.

# CHAPTER 11

# Arizona's Hidden Gems and Lesser-Known Treasures

---

*"The world is full of magical things, patiently waiting for our senses to grow sharper." – W.B. Yeats*

---

**Arizona may be famous for its iconic landmarks like the Grand Canyon and Monument Valley. Still, some of the most rewarding experiences in the state come from discovering its hidden gems. These lesser-known treasures are where the soul of Arizona truly shines.**

## Exploring Arizona's Caves and Natural Formations

Lava River Cave in Flagstaff is a mile-long lava tube formed around 700,000 years ago. Walking through it is like journeying into the Earth's core.

Another remarkable spot is Colossal Cave Mountain Park near Tucson. This dry cave system, used for centuries by Native Americans, is a treasure trove of history and geology. The guided tour takes you through chambers adorned with stalactites, stalagmites, and flowstone formations.

Kartchner Caverns State Park is a must-visit. Discovered in 1974 but kept secret for over a decade, this "living cave" is still growing its formations. The delicate formations, like soda straws and bacon ribbons, are a testament to the power of water and time.

## Hidden Hot Springs and Secluded Escapes

Castle Hot Springs is located in a secluded valley northwest of Phoenix. This historic resort, once frequented by the Rockefellers and Roosevelts, has been restored to offer a luxurious escape. The spring-fed pools are rich in minerals and surrounded by desert beauty, creating an idyllic, relaxing atmosphere.

If you're looking for something more rustic, the Verde Hot Springs near Camp Verde is a hidden gem with a fascinating history. Accessible only by a hike and a river crossing, these hot springs are remnants of a once-grand resort that burned down in the 1960s.

For a truly off-the-grid adventure, visit Sheep Bridge Hot Springs. Located in the rugged Tonto National Forest, these springs require a challenging drive and a short hike. However, the effort is well worth it. The springs are nestled along the Verde River, offering stunning views of the surrounding wilderness.

## Arizona's Quirky Roadside Stops

The Wigwam Motel in Holbrook is a Route 66 icon, with its teepee-shaped rooms that transport you back to the golden age of road trips. Staying here is like living in a postcard from the 1950s, complete with vintage cars parked outside each wigwam.

On another stretch of Route 66, you'll find the quirky town of Seligman, the inspiration for the Pixar movie Cars. This tiny town celebrates roadside Americana with retro diners, souvenir shops, and colorful murals honoring its heritage.

## Arizona Hidden Gem Bucketlist

### 1. Sedona's Red Rock State Park

Sedona's Red Rock State Park, where the trails are short, flat, and scenic. The Eagle's Nest Loop offers breathtaking views, while the family-oriented nature center hosts interactive programs.

**2. Wind Cave Trail in Usery Mountain Regional Park**

The Wind Cave Trail in Usery Mountain Regional Park is a 3-mile round-trip hike perfect for families, with a gradual incline and stunning desert views. At the trail's end, you're rewarded with a natural alcove that kids will love to explore.

**3. Tombstone Courthouse State Historic Park**

The Tombstone Courthouse offers a quieter and more introspective view of history. With exhibits that bring to life stories of the Wild West, it's a hidden gem for history buffs.

**4. The Little Colorado River Gorge**

The Little Colorado River Gorge offers a fantastic spot to witness nature's raw power while reflecting on Arizona's landscapes' untouched beauty.

**5. Crown King**

Tucked high in the Bradshaw Mountains, Crown King offers a refreshing escape from the desert heat. This quaint mountain town is perfect for a weekend retreat.

**6. Arizona Science Center**

The Science Center in Phoenix offers hands-on exhibits to the planetarium shows; this museum is a playground for curious kids.

**7. Pima Air & Space Museum**

Pima Air & Space Museum in Tucson is a sprawling complex with over 400 aircraft, including a retired Air Force One.

# CHAPTER 12

# Arizona's Lakes and Water Activities

*"Adopt the pace of nature: her secret is patience." – Ralph Waldo Emerson*

**When most people think of Arizona, they imagine arid deserts and towering cacti. But Arizona is also a haven for water lovers. With its glittering lakes and riverfront escapes, the state offers countless opportunities to cool off, unwind, and reconnect with nature.**

Arizona, known for its rugged deserts and breathtaking canyons, holds a hidden secret—pristine lakes tucked away like oases in an arid landscape.

**1. Lake Powell – Adventure on the Edge of Sandstone**

Spanning across Arizona and Utah, Lake Powell is more than a destination—it's an epic odyssey waiting to unfold. Explore its maze of canyons by kayak, marvel at Rainbow Bridge or simply anchor your boat in a secluded cove. Houseboat rentals create the ideal home base for the ultimate adventure.

- Kayaking through Antelope Canyon
- Houseboat rentals for multi-day stays
- Jet skiing against iconic sandstone backdrops

**2. Lake Havasu – Where Thrill Meets Tranquility**

Known as a haven for water sports and spring break revelry, Lake Havasu also offers secluded pockets of calm. Take a leap of courage on a wakeboard or slow things down with a serene paddleboarding session. And don't forget to visit the London Bridge—transported from England stone by stone as a symbol of what's possible when you think big.

- Wakeboarding and jet skiing thrills
- Paddleboarding at sunrise
- Strolling across the historic London Bridge

**3. Saguaro Lake – Serenity Amongst the Cacti**

Tucked amidst the Tonto National Forest, Saguaro Lake creates a stunning juxtaposition of verdant water and towering desert cacti. Glide through its canyon walls in a kayak or set out on a fishing boat to reconnect with stillness.

- Fishing for bass and catfish
- Kayaking alongside towering cliffs
- The Desert Belle Tour Boat for panoramic lake views

**4. Lake Pleasant – For the Free-Spirited Explorer**

Set just outside Phoenix, Lake Pleasant is the perfect spot for those who seek both adventure and reprieve from the sun. Brave the waves on a rented speedboat, hike the nearby trails, or wind down with a picnic by the water's edge.

- Boating and jet skiing
- Hiking on the Pipeline Canyon Trail
- Stargazing by the lakeshore

**5. Roosevelt Lake – A Hidden Gem Worth Finding**

A quieter treasure, Roosevelt Lake is often overlooked—and that's its charm. Situated amongst rolling hills and distant peaks, this expansive lake offers pristine waters and a sense of calm that lets you breathe a little deeper.

- Scenic drives across Roosevelt Dam
- Fishing tournaments for enthusiasts
- Shaded camping spots under the warm Arizona sky

**6. Canyon Lake – A Smaller Lake with Big Charm**

With dramatic canyon walls framing its shimmering waters, Canyon Lake provides visitors with landscapes that stir the soul. Cruise along the Dolly Steamboat or challenge yourself to a paddle through its winding coves.

- Scenic boat rides on the Dolly Steamboat
- Cliffside kayaking for unforgettable adventures
- Spotting wildlife like bighorn sheep and bald eagles

**7. Patagonia Lake – The Perfect Southwestern Getaway**

Nestled near Patagonia, this lake is for those who crave a quiet escape. It's a place for paddleboards, reflections on an anchored canoe, or afternoons spent picnicking under lush mesquites.

- Canoeing through pockets of still water
- Birdwatching along the lakefront trails
- Day-use cabanas for a family retreat

## Arizona's Stunning Smaller Lakes Bucketlist

**1. Watson Lake (Prescott)**

Surrounded by striking granite boulders, Watson Lake is a kayaking and paddleboarding paradise.

**2. Lynx Lake (Prescott)**

Nestled in the heart of the Prescott National Forest, Lynx Lake offers opportunities for fishing, canoeing, and birdwatching.

**3. Lake Patagonia (Patagonia)**

Enveloped by rolling hills, this hidden gem feels like a retreat. The lake is popular for boating, fishing, and even nighttime stargazing.

**4. Fool Hollow Lake (Show Low)**

A scenic escape in the White Mountains, Fool Hollow Lake is perfect for those who want to boat, kayak, and camp.

**5. Bartlett Lake (Tonto National Forest)**

While Bartlett Lake might not be as photographed as the famous Lake Powell, it's a quiet haven for water enthusiasts. Swimming, jet skiing, and fishing are popular here.

**6. Blue Ridge Reservoir (Coconino National Forest)**

This secluded lake feels like it's hidden from the rest of the world.

**7. Saguaro Lake (Tonto National Forest)**

For a blend of desert charm and aquatic fun, Saguaro Lake is unbeatable. Rent a boat or join a guided fishing expedition, and be prepared to see breathtaking views of saguaros.

**8. Canyon Lake (Apache Junction)**

A quick trip from the bustling Phoenix area, Canyon Lake surprises visitors with its dramatic cliffs and clear waters. The Desert Belle boat cruise is a must-do if you want to learn about the area's history.

### 9. Goldwater Lake (Prescott)

Tucked in the forests surrounding Prescott, Goldwater Lake is a small, serene spot for picnics, kayaking, or light hikes.

# CHAPTER 13

# Arizona's Dark Skies and Stargazing Spots

*"The stars don't look bigger, but they do look brighter from here." – Sally Ride*

**In Arizona, the night skies here are like no other. Arizona is a haven for stargazers, offering some of the clearest and most stunning night skies in the world.**

If you're looking for the ultimate stargazing experience, Arizona has plenty to offer. A favorite spot is Kitt Peak National Observatory, located about an hour southwest of Tucson. Perched atop a mountain at 6,880 feet, Kitt Peak is home to one of the largest collections of telescopes in the world. Guided tours and nighttime programs make it a must-visit for both beginners and seasoned astronomers.

Another gem is Lowell Observatory in Flagstaff. This historic site is where Pluto was discovered in 1930, and its connection to astronomical history adds an extra layer of magic to any visit. On a clear night, the observatory's advanced telescopes allow you to see details of distant galaxies.

For those who prefer a more remote experience, Chiricahua National Monument is an excellent choice. Nestled in southeastern Arizona, this park's rugged terrain and minimal light pollution make it a stargazer's paradise.

Then there's Grand Canyon National Park, which offers breathtaking views both day and night. During the annual Grand Canyon Star Party, amateur and professional astronomers gather to share their knowledge and telescopes with visitors.

## Tips for Planning Your Arizona Stargazing Trip

Timing is everything. The best stargazing conditions occur during a new moon when the sky is at its darkest. Use a lunar calendar to plan your trip around this phase, and check the weather forecast for clear skies. Location is just as important. While Arizona's urban areas are beautiful, their light pollution can hinder your ability to see faint stars and celestial objects. Aim for remote locations like national parks, observatories, or dark sky parks. Apps like Dark Sky Finder can help you pinpoint areas with minimal light interference.

## Arizona's Dark Sky Communities and Parks

Arizona is a leader in the dark sky movement, with several communities and parks dedicated to preserving the night sky for future generations. Visiting these places is not only a treat for stargazers but also a way to support efforts to combat light pollution.

One of the most notable dark sky communities is Flagstaff, the world's first International Dark Sky City. Here, you'll find a commitment to protecting the night sky that's evident in the city's lighting ordinances and public outreach programs. Flagstaff's residents take pride in their starry skies, and it shows.

Another standout is Sedona, known for its stunning red rock landscapes and equally breathtaking night skies. The city's strict lighting codes ensure that visitors can enjoy an unobstructed view of the stars.

Arizona is also home to numerous dark sky parks, including Kartchner Caverns State Park and Oracle State Park. These parks offer designated stargazing areas, educational programs, and even overnight camping options.

## Celestial Events and Astronomy Festivals

One of the most exciting aspects of stargazing in Arizona is the opportunity to witness celestial events and attend astronomy festivals. From meteor showers to eclipses, there's always something happening in the sky.

The Perseid meteor shower, which peaks in August, is one of the most spectacular events of the year. With dozens of meteors streaking across the sky every hour, it's a sight that never fails to inspire awe.

Another must-see event is a total lunar eclipse. During these rare occurrences, the moon takes on a reddish hue, earning it the nickname "blood moon." Watching this phenomenon from the Arizona desert is an otherworldly experience that you won't want to miss.

Arizona also hosts several astronomy festivals, including the Grand Canyon Star Party and the Arizona Science and Astronomy Expo. These events bring together astronomy enthusiasts of all ages for telescope viewings, workshops, and guest lectures.

## **Star Gazing Bucketlist**

1. Bright Angel Point
2. Oracle State Park
3. Buffalo Park
4. Lowell Observatory
5. Grand Canyon-Parashant National Monument
6. Kartchner Caverns State Park
7. Kitt Peak National Observatory (Hidden Trails) - Tohono O'odham Reservation, AZ
8. Chiricahua National Monument - Southeastern Arizona
9. Alamo Lake State Park - Western Arizona
10. Homolovi State Park - Winslow, AZ

# CONCLUSION

---

***"We travel not to escape life, but for life not to escape us." – Anonymous***

---

Arizona is a reminder of how vast and diverse our world is. Its deserts, mountains, and canyons show the power of nature, while its towns and cities showcase the creativity and resilience of the people who call this state home. By exploring Arizona, you've become a part of its story, and it has become a part of yours.

# BONUS 1

# Top Bucket List Places to Visit in Arizona

## Must-See Natural Wonders

1. **Grand Canyon National Park**—Stand in awe of one of the World's Seven Natural Wonders.
2. **Antelope Canyon**—Walkthrough sandstone slot canyons sculpted by time and water.
3. **Horseshoe Bend**—Witness the dramatic curve of the Colorado River from above.
4. **Petrified Forest National Park**—Explore ancient trees that have turned into stunning, multicolored stone.
5. **Sedona's Red Rock Formations**—Be mesmerized by crimson landscapes that have inspired generations.
6. **Monument Valley**—Iconic vistas that have graced countless films and postcards.
7. **Havasu Falls**—Discover turquoise cascades hidden deep within the Grand Canyon.
8. **The Wave**—Marvel at surreal sandstone waves (requires a permit, but worth every effort).
9. **Saguaro National Park**—Stroll among towering saguaro cacti in this desert utopia.
10. **Meteor Crater**—Visit a perfectly preserved impact crater from 50,000 years ago.
11. **Desert Botanical Garden**—Walk through a desert garden with 50,000 plants spread over 140 acres.

12. **Grand Canyon Village**—Visit a village dating back to the 20th century.
13. **Camelback Mountain**—Hike and climb a formation resembling a camel's hump.

## Adventures for Thrill-Seekers

14. **Rim-to-Rim Hike of the Grand Canyon**—Conquer one of the nation's most iconic hikes.
15. **Kayaking on Lake Powell**—Paddle through hidden canyons and crystal-clear waters.
16. **Hot Air Balloon Ride Over Phoenix**—See the Sonoran Desert from the sky at dawn.
17. **Stargazing and Astronomy Whitewater Rafting the Colorado River**—Feel the intensity of nature in the Grand Canyon's roaring rapids.
18. **Skydiving Over Arizona's Desert**—Get your adrenaline fix paired with unbeatable views.

## Iconic Cultural Landmarks

19. **Taliesin West**—Tour Frank Lloyd Wright's architectural masterpiece.
20. **Mission San Xavier del Bac**—Admire this stunning 18th-century Spanish mission outside Tucson.
21. **Old Town Scottsdale**—Shop artisan crafts and experience cowboy heritage.
22. **The Heard Museum**—Dive deep into Native American art and culture.
23. **Route 66 (Winslow, Arizona)**—Stand on a corner and relive the magic of this historic highway.

## Stargazing & Astronomy

24. **Lowell Observatory**—Discover the stars at the site where Pluto was first identified.
25. **Kitt Peak National Observatory**—Peer into the universe from one of the world's finest telescope facilities.
26. **Sedona's Night Sky**— International Dark-Sky Community? Prepare to lose yourself in an infinite blanket of stars.
27. **Flagstaff Dark Skies**—Officially certified as a dark-sky city for prime stargazing.
28. **Meteor Shower in the Desert**—Plan your trip during the Perseids for an unforgettable night.

## Unique Local Experiences

29. **Tombstone**—Step back in time in this famed Wild West town.
30. **Bisbee**—Wander through an artistic community housed within a charming mining town.
31. **Arizona Wine Country (Verde Valley)**—Sip local vintages while enjoying pastoral landscapes.
32. **Santa Cruz Chili & Spice Co.**—Indulge in the rich culinary traditions of the Southwest.
33. **Sunset Crater Volcano National Monument**—Explore the lava fields of Arizona's volcanic past.

## Awe-Inspiring Road Trips

34. **Apache Trail**—Drive a scenic dirt road adventure past lakes, canyons, and cliffside views.
35. **Vermilion Cliffs National Monument**—Feel dwarfed by towering sandstone cliffs.

36. **Mogollon Rim**—Travel along this plateau's edge for unparalleled vistas.
37. **Jerome's Skyway**—Cruise through Arizona's famous "ghost town turned art hub."
38. **Chiricahua National Monument**—Take in a land of sky-high, precariously balanced rock spires.
39. **Monument Valley**—Take a surreal drive through towering red sandstone formations.
40. **Sedona's Red Rock Scenic Byway**—Drive this route through Sedona's glowing red cliffs and buttes.
41. **Petrified Forest National Park**— Drive through fossilized trees and vibrant badlands.
42. **Mount Lemmon Scenic Byway**—Drive this 27-mile road from desert landscapes to alpine forests.
43. **Lake Powell and Glen Canyon**—See where water meets sandstone, creating breathtaking scenic contrasts.

## Off-the-Beaten-Path Gems

44. **Canyon de Chelly National Monument**—Explore this sacred Navajo site with towering canyon walls.
45. **Tumacácori National Historical Park**—Visit these preserved Spanish mission ruins.
46. **Kartchner Caverns State Park**—Step into Arizona's best-preserved underground caves.
47. **Organ Pipe Cactus National Monument**—Walk among rare cacti on Mexico's border.
48. **Essence of Tranquility**—Explore a hot springs retreat offering six mineral-rich pools.

## Wellness & Reflection

49. **Sedona's Vortex Hikes**—Recharge at one of the city's spiritual energy spots.
50. **Page's Lake Powell Paddleboarding**—Find serenity skimming across still waters.
51. **A Day at Marble Canyon Ranch**—Relax amid spectacular views paired with horseback riding or fly fishing.

# BONUS 2

# Taste Arizona Recipes

## FRY BREAD

YIELDS: 4-6 | PREP TIME: 15 minutes | REST TIME: 10 minutes | COOK TIME: 12 minutes

### INGREDIENTS

- 2 cups all-purpose flour, plus more for dusting
- 1 ½ teaspoons baking powder
- 1 teaspoon salt
- 2 ½ tablespoons vegetable or canola oil, plus more for frying
- 1 ½–2 cups warm water

### INSTRUCTIONS

1. Combine the flour, baking powder, and salt in a large mixing bowl. Mix with your hands.
2. Create a well in the center and pour in the oil.
3. Slowly add the water while mixing the dough by hand until it comes together into a ball.
4. Transfer the dough to a lightly floured work surface and knead for a few minutes. Do not overwork—it should be smooth and soft.
5. Return the dough to the bowl, cover with a towel, and let it rest for 30 minutes.

6. Divide the dough into six equal portions and roll each into a ball.
7. Heat 1–2 inches of oil in a deep skillet to 350°F.
8. Roll each dough ball flat, then stretch and pat between both palms until about 6 inches in diameter. Use your hands to create a few small tears in the dough to prevent excessive puffing.
9. Fry each 6-inch dough disc for 2–3 minutes per side or until golden brown.
10. Carefully remove the fry bread from the oil and place it on a paper towel-lined platter to drain excess oil.
11. Repeat with the remaining dough.
12. Serve as desired.

**NOTES**

- Fry bread dough is hard to mess up. Add flour in small increments if it's too sticky and difficult to handle. If it's too dry, add more water.
- There are many ways to enjoy fry bread. Try making a Navajo taco by topping it with meat, lettuce, tomato, shredded cheese, and olives, or serve it with a scoop of ice cream and stewed apples or peaches.
- Fry bread can be stored in an airtight container at room temperature for 1–2 days or refrigerated for up to a week.
- For freezer storage, individually wrap each piece in plastic, place it in a freezer bag, and freeze for up to 3 months.

## CHIMICHANGAS

SERVES: 6 | PREP TIME: 45 minutes | COOK TIME: 2 hours and 10 minutes | COOL TIME: 15 minutes

### INGREDIENTS

#### Protein

- 3 ½ pounds beef chuck roast or bone-in chicken breast halves
- 1 tablespoon kosher salt
- ½ teaspoon ground cumin
- ½ teaspoon black pepper
- ½ teaspoon garlic powder
- 4 cups beef or chicken broth
- 2 dried chipotle chiles, stems and seeds removed
- 2 guajillo chiles, stems and seeds removed
- ½ cup tomato purée
- Juice of 1 lemon
- 2 tablespoons neutral oil
- 2 jalapeño peppers, stems removed and sliced
- 5 garlic cloves, peeled and sliced
- 3 bay leaves
- 1 teaspoon dried oregano
- 6 burrito-size flour tortillas
- 16 ounces shredded cheese (consider a blend of Monterey Jack and cheddar)
- Neutral oil for frying

**Optional Toppings**

- Mexican crema
- Avocado slices
- Chopped tomato
- Olives
- Chopped romaine lettuce

## INSTRUCTIONS

**Braise:**

1. Preheat the oven to 250°F.
2. Pat the meat or poultry dry, then season with salt, cumin, black pepper, and garlic powder. Set aside.
3. Bring the broth to a boil, then add the dried chiles. Let them steep for 10–15 minutes to soften.
4. Transfer the broth and rehydrated chiles to a blender with the tomato purée and lemon juice. Blend until smooth.
5. Heat a Dutch oven over medium-high heat. Add the oil.
6. Sear the beef or chicken on both sides, then pour in the braising liquid. Add the sliced jalapeño, garlic, bay leaves, and oregano.
7. Cover with a lid, transfer to the oven, and braise for 2–3 hours.
8. Remove the beef (or chicken) from the pot and let it cool for 15 minutes.
9. Shred with two forks. Remove the skin and bones from the breast halves if you made chicken.

**Assembly:**

1. Place a tortilla flat on a clean work surface. Add meat and cheese, then tightly wrap the burrito. You may use toothpicks to keep the burrito intact while frying.
2. Repeat with the remaining tortillas, meat, and cheese.

**Frying:**

1. Heat 2 inches of oil in a deep skillet or deep fryer to 375°F.
2. Working with 1–2 burritos at a time, fry for 3–4 minutes, flipping halfway through. Place on paper towels to drain excess oil.
3. Repeat with the remaining burritos.
4. Plate and serve chimichangas as desired with any optional toppings.

**NOTES**

- If you prefer not to fry, brush the chimichangas with oil and bake at 450°F for 8–10 minutes.
- Store leftovers in an airtight container and refrigerate for 3–4 days. Alternatively, you can individually wrap and freeze for up to 2 months.
- To reheat previously fried chimichangas that have been refrigerated or frozen, microwave for 30 seconds (or 1 minute if frozen), then transfer to a 350°F oven for 8–10 minutes.
- You don't have to fry all the burritos at once. Assemble and freeze them as instructed above, then fry as needed.

## CHEESE CRISP

SERVES: 1 | PREP TIME: 5 minutes | COOK TIME: 8 minutes

### INGREDIENTS

- 1 medium flour tortilla (8-10 inches); use the thinnest you can find (Guerrero Riquísimas are a great choice)
- ¼ cup shredded cheddar cheese
- ¼ cup shredded Monterey Jack cheese
- 1 teaspoon unsalted butter or margarine, softened
- 1-2 tablespoons chopped roasted Anaheim chilies, fresh jalapeños, or canned jalapeños (if using)

### INSTRUCTIONS

1. Preheat the oven to 425°F.
2. Spread the softened butter or margarine on one side of the tortilla. Place it on a cookie sheet, buttered side up. Bake for 3-4 minutes or until the tortilla starts to brown.
3. Evenly sprinkle the cheese over the tortilla, ensuring the surface is covered. Top with the chilies, if using.
4. Return to the oven and bake for 5-7 minutes or until the cheese is melted and bubbly.
5. Cut into wedges and enjoy.

### NOTES

- The recipe can be scaled up as needed.

## CHOCOLATE TAMALES

YIELDS: 14 tamales | PREP TIME: 1 hour | COOK TIME: 35 minutes | REST TIME: 15 minutes

### INGREDIENTS

- 16-18 corn husks
- Boiling water
- 2 cups masa harina
- ½ cup granulated sugar
- ⅓ cup Dutch-processed cocoa powder
- 1 teaspoon baking powder
- ¼-½ teaspoon ground cinnamon
- ¼ teaspoon salt
- 1 cup butter or margarine, softened
- 1 teaspoon vanilla extract
- 1 ¾ cups whole milk, warmed
- 1 ¾ cups semi-sweet chocolate chips or Nutella

### INSTRUCTIONS

**Prepare the corn husks:**

1. Add the corn husks to a large bowl and cover with boiling water. Soak for 30 minutes to soften.

**Prepare the dough:**

2. Meanwhile, in a mixing bowl, whisk together the masa harina, sugar, cocoa powder, baking powder, cinnamon, and salt.
3. Add the softened butter or margarine and mix until the dough is crumbly. You can use your hands, similar to making pie dough, to help distribute the fat evenly.
4. Pour in the vanilla extract, then gradually add the warm milk, mixing by hand or with an electric mixer until the dough is soft, smooth, and slightly sticky. You may not need all the milk.
5. Cover the dough with a damp towel and rest for 10 minutes.

**Assembly and steaming:**

6. While the dough rests, rinse the soaked corn husks and pat them dry. Also, prepare a steamer pot by adding 1-2 inches of water and fitting it with a steamer basket.
7. Lay a corn husk smooth side up, with the narrow end at the bottom. Place about 3 tablespoons of chocolate masa dough in the center.
8. Spread the dough evenly with a spoon, then add 1-2 tablespoons of chocolate chips or Nutella in the center.
9. Fold the right side of the husk toward the center, then fold the left side over it so they overlap.
10. Fold the narrow end up toward the wide end, ensuring you don't squeeze too hard to prevent the dough from spilling out.
11. Repeat with the remaining dough and filling.
12. Line the steamer basket with any extra corn husks and carefully place the tamales inside, with the open ends facing up.
13. Cover the pot with a tight-fitting lid and bring the water to a boil. Once bubbling, reduce the heat to low and steam for 35-

45 minutes. The tamales are done when the masa is set, pulls away from the husks, and does not stick.

14. Remove the tamales from the pot and let them rest for 15-20 minutes before serving.
15. Serve and enjoy!

**NOTES**

- If some of your corn husks are too small, overlap two and proceed to assemble the tamales.
- If you don't have corn husks, use parchment paper as an alternative.

## PRICKLY PEAR SORBET

SERVES: 4-6 | PREP TIME: 15 minutes | FREEZE TIME: 6 hours

**INGREDIENTS**

- 3 pounds prickly pears
- 2 ounces fresh raspberries
- ½ cup simple syrup
- Juice of 1 lime

**INSTRUCTIONS**

1. While wearing rubber gloves to protect your hands, wash the prickly pears and use paper towels to rub off any fuzz.
2. Cut the prickly pears lengthwise, then scoop the flesh and seeds into a blender.
3. Add the simple syrup and lime juice to the blender as well.

4. Blend until smooth. Taste and adjust as needed, adding more simple syrup or lime juice if desired.
5. Strain the purée through a fine-mesh sieve. Discard any seeds and pulp.
6. Transfer to a freezer-safe container and freeze for 6-8 hours.
7. Dip an ice cream scoop in warm water, scoop the sorbet into dessert glasses, and enjoy!

## NOTES

- To make simple syrup, combine equal parts sugar and water in a saucepan (1:1 ratio). Bring to a boil, stirring until the sugar dissolves. Remove from heat and let cool completely before using.
- Leftover simple syrup can be stored in an airtight container in the refrigerator for 3-4 weeks.

Made in the USA
Monee, IL
15 March 2026